"Few contemporary poetry boo
epic, rhapsodic, prophetic a voice
here the journey takes us through Jamaica of the poet's childhood to
ways of perceiving the interior – in museums, galleries, art studios
of the world. This formally inventive book is a singing in defense
of deeper contemplation. Having seen the 'surreal landscape of
history's graveyard' and understood 'what it means to be a refugee in
your own country' the poet gives us wisdom. Through McCallum's
clarity of perspective, her musical, memorable clarity, the soul stands
apart, sees and is seen. With unrelenting honesty, here is a book that
proposes we take a step back from the shallowness of our age and
open our eyes – as the many painters and landscapes the poet finds
herself in front of do – to behold the world that is ours. Behold.
Behold. This is a beautiful, soul-making book."

— Ilya Kaminsky

"In Behold, Shara McCallum moves as a curator would, assembling
a museum of migration's afterlives – art haunted by the spectral
presence of those of us grappling with migration's wake. In her
poetics of looking, which is to say reverence, she listens to these
works the way Tina Campt teaches us to listen to images: not only
for what they show, but for their sonic frequencies – for what hums
beneath, what whispers, what reverberates. Each poem is an object
lesson in the root of curating, curare – to care: to gather what has
been abandoned, to tend to grief through beauty, to attune to those
silenced in the archives – the laborers in cane fields, the children left
behind, the ancestors bound by red threads. McCallum also listens as
others witness – the security guards, so often unseen in their quiet
labor, who imbue their favorite works of art with their own lived
histories. To behold art shaped by migration is to witness both beauty
and wound, rupture and repair. And yet, in its poetics of migration,
Behold teaches us not all of migration's wounds must be made visible;
at times, looking and listening closely means resting with opacity."

— Grace Aneiza Ali, Curator

"Shara McCallum's *Behold* is the kind of book that first stunned me into the abiding love I have for language. At once mystical, political, and lyrical, these poems redraw the boundaries of what we might consider the limits of human insight. Poems like these remind us that, if there is ever to be a fully realized awakening in terms of our relationship to history, we need poetry."

— Tim Seibles

"Shara McCallum's Behold moves through museums and galleries with a spirit of wonder and attention. These poems do what the strongest ekphrastic work does: they respond to art without explaining it, making something new in the space between looking and feeling.

The collection traces a life lived in relation to visual culture – from the Impressionist reproductions beloved by the poet's grandmother, to art history classrooms, and conversations with artists and gallery assistants. This autobiographical thread gives the book its depth and mastery, as the speaker's inward life unfolds alongside the art.

These poems are fiercely intelligent and musically alert, attentive to seeing as a form of thought. At the centre of the collection is Jamaica, the poet's birthplace, a steady point of return."

— Hannah Lowe

BEHOLD

Poems

ALSO BY SHARA McCALLUM

SHARA McCALLUM

BEHOLD

PEEPAL TREE

First published in Great Britain in 2026
Peepal Tree Press Ltd
17 King's Avenue
Leeds LS6 1QS
UK

ISBN 13: 9781845236113

Supported using public funding by
ARTS COUNCIL
ENGLAND

for Sally Kathleen Norris DePass, the OG
&
Steve, Rachel, and Naomi

CONTENTS

Behold, I have come — in the volume of the book
it is written of me — To do your will.

— Hebrews 10:7

PASSAGE

moving still: processional crossings, Marta Gentilucci

I have come
not to beg nor barter but to enter.

                                          Who are you seeking?

The past
opens and opens, fleshing me
with loss.
I descend
to find my way,
I who am
haunted and a haunting.

                             What are you willing to abandon?

In the before, I continue:
a woman carrying on with the dishes,
the dusting, the sweeping.
But here, I am the voice of the petitioner.
Dearest, who was once of earth,
Dearest, whose departure has cleft me,
Dearest, who was my country,
my soil, my sun and sky,
every migration
is a bird taking wing.

                                 Is this the place you seek?

Returned to the house of memory,
I take winding roads up into hills.
At one street I slow, searching
for the familiar gate
to tell me I've reached. But thickets
spring up, blocking my way.
I turn to find another path,

following again
until road dissolves to mist.

And if at last I arrive,
will I find you in that room
with every window like the soul
flung open and flooded
with sounds of the distant sea.

And if I spill
out into the yard, will she be still
there, the child who was me
set down in the grass,
watching the stars blinkering
on and off, their light burning
with the knowledge of death.

Is this the place you seek?

In that field I repeat
the part of myself
who believes she can stall this,
calling and calling her throat hoarse.
But you do not hear. You do not
look back but keep walking, the distance
between us widening
all night into dawn.

I want to spirit her
from this rift. I want to lift her
out of this moment and alight on any other.
But here, no bird can take wing.
No path rises up to meet my feet.
Now I have brought us
again to this place, I wade through
grasses swelling like waves,
now in this field again

I remember
as each time before
I remember
why I cannot stay and why
I must abandon you here.
At this threshold,
your last breathing –
in my ears –
is a claw dragging itself
across.

How will you carry this?

I will have to use the flowers to address you.
Wild-blooming frangipani (your cloying scent marks me).
Pointillist-starred ixora (I braid you into my hair).
Indigo-blue plumbago (you obliterate the sky).
Lignum vitae (you foretell all histories).
Roses that grow ragged along the shore (stay with me).

How will you return to the living?

Called back by the susurrating wind and sea.
Called back by the roots of my hair, dirt
beneath my nails, the body's sweat and stink.
Called back by their voices, yours
still clenched in my fist. Called back
to all that is matter, bone, and skin,
what fragment of you survives in me
as I open my mouth to speak?

∞ ∞ ∞

as the soul is a mirror before / painting it is a home

—— Medbh McGuckian

∞ ∞ ∞

PASTORAL
Crop Time, Albert Huie

This is the Jamaica you were not born
into. In this field the artist has layered
bodies of labourers, hefting wrapped
bundles of sugar cane, lifting these
onto bull-drawn carts. Other men raise
machetes as if in choreographed motion.
Others in unison hunch over earth,
digging. Only one figure on this canvas
faces front, holding a reed to his lips.
You want to believe he is the piper.
Behind him soars a grey cluster
of buildings, smokestacks, smoke
wreathing up to the sky. The smell,
that burning is in you still.

SNOW

The first museum I ever visited was the Metropolitan Museum of Art. I was twenty years old, and it was also my first trip to New York City and first time seeing snow. Growing up mainly in my grandparent's home after migrating to Miami, I'd been exposed to visual art through my grandmother's loves. Anyone who entered our small townhouse in Kendall joked it was Sally's Gallery. She hung framed prints of paintings, many by French Impressionists and other so-called Masters, the reproductions of which were sold in art shops she frequented in South Florida. These filled-up every inch of the walls, including the ones in the bedroom my sisters and I shared. I don't know how many hours of my adolescence I spent consciously or without thought absorbing those artists' works. But, no wonder, when I went to the Met, I made a beeline for the Impressionists. I remember standing in front of a Renoir and realising the obvious: how different the textures and colours of the image were in person. I remember I kept running back and forth between the painting and the oversized windows that looked out onto Central Park to watch the snow that had begun falling.

THE COLOUR OF DEPARTURE
Banner Project, Sheida Soleimani

is a bright blue
suitcase with silver
buckles metal flaps
that click open and snap
shut this leather case
gives away
the year of travel
I know intimately
this luggage
the very sort that lugged
my sisters' and my little clothes
trinkets and other hastily
gathered family
possessions across borders

SELF-PORTRAIT

At this point, I don't know what in me is Jamaican
versus American. Or, reaching further back,
Trinidadian, Venezuelan, African, Scottish, English...
you get the drift. I thought *every mickle mek a muckle*
was from Kingston soil sprung, until in Edinburgh
I heard it in the mouth of a Scotsman. For years, I filed
my grandmother's *doudou* as Patwa, failing to detect
Trini-French patois in her mongrel dialect.

How do you say aluminum or Armageddon? Ah, for me,
there interposes an extra syllable, an invisible *I*.
And why should any one I matter? is a fair question.
Only because the alternative is worse. And since
we're on the topic of the singular, about this subject:
she's awfully tired of being parsed to see if she's a fraud.

HOW OFTEN DO YOU RETURN

Whenever I eat porridge or drink tea.
Whenever the refrain *poor me Israelites* sounds
and somehow calls up castor oil, gentian violet,
iodine, mercurochrome – all the remedies for all
that could possibly ail you my mother knew.
Anytime I meet someone whose *ha-low*
are the two syllables it takes for me to suss out
they too are every day returning, who like me
says *fi true* and *yeah man* yet keeps marvelling –
Yu really from Kingston? Everywhere I go
where I see a mountain, even lickle hill rising,
am nearish a river or semblance of sea.
Predictable, kinda pathetic. I get it. But true.
Just as when night plays the fool
and a half-way-sorta-warmish breeze sends
late-summer's flowers climbing ladders of air.
Is so my mind trellises. Is so
trickery abounds, when our one heart
is ragged, and the other runs roughshod over it.

HOW TO SEE

When I decided to become a poet, it was after letting go the paths
– medicine or, if that failed, law – I was expected to be on by
attending university. Only then, when I saw I was actually going to
throw my life away, did I take two art classes.

In the first, introduction to drawing, I worked with pen, pencil,
and charcoal on paper. I spent hours absorbed by such assignments
as reproducing a vase of flowers without lifting my hand from the
page. My instructor was encouraging, but no matter how he sugar-
coated his feedback, I knew I was not a natural. Bemoaning this to
a friend with a gift for painting but who, unlike me, had continued
on the medical school track, I was greeted with her usual acerbic
wit, "You can sing, dance, write, and act. I'm sorry, you can't
have it all." But I have always wanted to have it all and kept trying
to close the gap between desire and dexterity. In the end, the
only project with which I felt an iota of success was when told to
charcoal an entire sheet, then use my eraser to 'draw', training my
attention on the interplay of shadow and light.

The second was an advanced art history class I chose because the
time period it covered included a few of the European painters
(Impressionists) whose works I loved and, as an English major, I
thought I'd find interpretation of text to be in my wheelhouse. As it
turned out, the sheer volume of memorisation the classwork entailed
didn't further endear me to the art. After the course ended, I sadly
washed out all the details – in which museums works were held, the
year each was finished, etc. Even more depressing, when it came
time for me to engage as an art critic in my writing, I was humbled.
Every field boasts its own lexicon and methodology and, without
preliminary work in art history, I too-late realised I was in over my
head. My professor, not so inclined as my drawing instructor had
been to gentle critique, plainly and continually reminded me of my
lack. Every essay was returned with a variation on this theme: *Shara,
you need to learn how to see what the artist is asking and stop imposing your
own desires unto the art.*

THE COLOUR OF GRIEF
Street Scene, David Pottinger

here is the moon's caustic gaze
here a street at night rent
by shadows a road morphing
into a river coming down
from a mountain that leads
to nowhere to place
myself in this scene is
to cannibalise and be consumed
where even would I stand
and not be burnished by
the street lamp's grey haze where
could my face peer out but
from one of the lightless windows
in one of these darkened houses

AT THE SEA
The Tragedy, Pablo Picasso

The tragedy remains unspoken.
Yet we can see it in the adults'
hunched shoulders, their arms
wrapping tightly their torsos. A trio:
this man, woman, and child stand
barefoot on the sand, white-foamed
waves approaching their feet.
The woman holds herself apart,
and I make of them a family,
attach to them a rift. Suffused
in greys and blues, the image
becomes a pall. The drawn faces
of man and woman, their gazes
at a downward pitch, reveal each
as stranded in their separate griefs.
When does it become impossible
to console? All of who we are
begins in disaster. And in the painting
the child's eyes are the ones open
to this fissured moment, a lifetime
spent trying will not unriddle.

THE STORM

Memory: Future, Howardena Pindell

All around us the air congregated.
Wind forced trees to submit,
their branches kneeling,
keeling and keening, as blue
drained itself from the sky, and ochre
and vermillion claimed dominion.
I read the signs – the birds
having fled, silence taking hold –
and clasped your hand into my own.
No home to which we could in time
return, we ran toward every arbour,
mistaking each one for harbour.
Inside that storm, I sought to be your
protector, I, who am no more.

IF YOU TOOK PHOTOS YOU COULD SEE MORE AND GET THROUGH FASTER

I'm given this advice from more than one well-intended museum guard when they observe me standing in front of an artwork, scribbling in my notebook, and query what I'm doing.

The phrase, "see more and get through faster," hits my ears the way "I did ___" (fill-in the blank with any famed site) sounded when I heard it from students I accompanied on a semester abroad some years back. Based in London, we toured that city and a handful of other European capitals, frequenting museums. I imagine the students were unthinkingly using this idiom, in the manner most of us do: shorthand for where we've travelled, what we've seen. Though it can become a sleight of hand, a way to establish status, flash our badge of having acquired certain kinds of culture. More so, I fear this language pushes us to experience art as an item on a to-do list, to be checked off.

When I go to a museum, I'm trying to slow down and take in as much as I have the capacity for truly seeing, which, as it turns out, isn't very much at all. The call for my rapt attention, placed on me *by* art or that *I've* placed on myself – it makes no difference who is the instigator – is what I've come for. No matter I'll never fully meet this demand, the attempt is hallowing.

I was raised Rastafarian and was a devout little girl before I came to America, before my father's death, before I stopped believing in God, all of which happened within a span of a few years in my late childhood. I've often thought it a strange phrase – *to lose one's faith* – as if it were a misplaced set of keys. But now, I think it precisely the right wording. I think, when as a child I indeed lost my faith, a part of my mind kept searching. When I enter a museum, it is as if that part, the one that still desires devotion and worship, has re-found its perch. When I look at art, I often feel I could weep.

PARABLE
Feeding the Fishes, John Dunkley

There is a story told of a woman
who would leave her home, her children
in their beds, to walk to the cliff ledge
jutting over the ravine. Night's face
shone on her sometimes, dredging her
in silver light, at other turns netting her
in its lack. Long dead, a tree stump
on the bank below sprouted a leaf,
each of its veins glowing. For a time,
she became this nightly walking
to the river to lean into the dark, feeding
the fishes she could not see clustering
on the surface. Her feet practicing
this path though there was no path.

WHEN NIGHT COMES IN ITS DARK CLOTHES

the threat of your death
stains me
like tea sieved
through cheesecloth
blooming its tannins

DOMESTIC INTERIOR

Pain enters through an open window
and you say it is the wind.

It marrows into beams, gutters
walls. Still you insist:

It is only a passing storm.
All while it seeps under your door —

long having eluded the watchman,
fallen asleep at his post — and floods

the whole damn house. Come daybreak,
you are a different kind of hostage now,

as it weeps into your bowl of porridge,
casts itself into the misshapen face

gleaming back at you from a tarnished spoon.
In time, you will make your bed

with this new order. In time,
you will simply make the bed and lie down.

FAIRYTALE
Hidden Forest, Lydia Panas

in the woods I lost sight of you
that moment you were caught
in branches that must have tangled
your hair and sent you tripping
over unseen roots thick undergrowth
of the forest floor denying us passage
in these woods without clearing
or sunlight gathering I have been
seeking the way to lay my body down
inside your shadow the umbra
of the child once laughing or if it be
your will my limbs will vine upon
fallen trees assuming their decay here
where for as long as forever I will stay

SELF-PORTRAIT: WINTER LANDSCAPE, 1997

through cracks in the stone foundation
entered drafts of air and mice
I could not bring myself to kill
so trapped them
in translucent boxes with a door
that swung only one way in
not meaning to but terrorising
them quickly dehydrating
their small bodies till I heard
frenzied scratching and hurried
to free them to the frozen fields
from which soon enough
they'd run back reentering
the warm cellar before
creeping up to the kitchen larder
and we'd begin again
all that winter as the house
seeped into me its damp
a feeling like the mucky pond
beyond the bay window
in front of which I often sat
watching accumulating branches
fallen leaves scumming its surface
imagining what lay beneath
the filmy water were fish
swimming in ever-slower circles
hovering under rocks and moss
skimming the tarn floor
while in the air above us all
icy clouds interred the sun

BUT WOULDN'T IT BE BETTER TO TAKE PHOTOS OF WHAT YOU'RE SEEING TO HELP YOU WRITE

Admittedly, my preferred process — to take notes in front of an artwork and later shape poems from those and memory — is a privileged one and not one I can always make happen. When a photograph is involved, it's usually one I've found in an art book or increasingly a digital reproduction, facsimiles created by photographers with far more skill than I possess.

Reproduction is largely what enabled my grandmother to cultivate a love of art, beginning with works she was taught to see as valuable and fanning out from there to her developing and trusting her own eye. But over the past decades, with many hours spent inside museums, I've witnessed a pretty dramatic shift in the role photography plays in how we engage with art.

My most visceral experience of this was ten years ago, when my family and I visited the Louvre. It was our first time going to Paris, and my husband and I were advised by everyone who'd ever been to the museum to have a game plan for tackling its overwhelming scope and maze-like construction. In advance, we let our daughters, then eleven and nine, each choose a piece to see. Our older picked *Mona Lisa*, having studied it in an art class the year before, and we began our visit by navigating to the room holding the painting.

Copies of art rarely convey actual size, but given the hoopla around this particular artwork, we were still surprised at its scale. *Mona Lisa* is teeny in real life. To get close enough to view it, my daughter and I had to wade through an army of people with cameras and selfie sticks raised high above their heads — a sight, we now know, as common as dirt at every famous museum, around every well-known piece of art.

When finally we managed to position ourselves in front of *Mona Lisa*, I asked my daughter what she thought. And though she tried to tell me and I tried to listen, all the while we were distracted by a woman who had been nudging me with her body and was now wildly gesticulating for me to move myself and my child out of her way, so she could take a picture of herself with the painting.

WILDING

Machetazo!, Bony Ramirez & *Blonde Dreams*, Alison Saar

you can take the girl out of the wilderness
you can strand her bewilder her for a time
you can even hang her upside down
in your rickety attempt to shake loose
the source of her power but you won't ever
disentangle the wilding from her
the force of a thousand suns unfurling
and hurling her toward the ground
you won't be able to erase the traces
of salt lacing her ravenous dreams
oh you can try unwebbing her feet
but the lizard in her will keep sunning
itself as the day is long and at nightfall
will crawl up your walls lurking
at the corners of your vision
goading you on while she thwarts
your every endeavour abandoning
her tail anything required of her
to keep eluding your capture

SELF-PORTRAIT: MIAMI, 1984

Salted by the sea & sweat – rivulets
running down my back & neck

& pooling in the creases
of my bent knees – I was slicked

to the seat of a car hurtling down US1.
After all day spent in sun,

over-radiated, overtired, & over-hungry,
my sisters & I had whined & whined

till our mother, harried & harangued
by us every day of her young life,

relented & agreed to stop at Dairy Queen,
trying to buy herself *just one moment of peace*.

Those were the days I went to bed with Armageddon
tucked beneath my pillow, not knowing

if nuclear annihilation would occur
before I'd wake again into this America

I was amassing, my adolescence
spent trying to unfrizz my hair, edging my body

around entrails of heat. Had it already begun
or was it just beginning, the real life

I wanted so desperately to claim.
Was it then, in that car with the windows

rolled down, the dark & humid air rushing in,
that I confused every cell of me for a galaxy

of dust, the aftertaste of ocean, sugar,
& girlhood on my tongue, compressed.

MAYBE A SELFIE

is an aesthetic project I don't understand because I don't typically take them don't use social media I share of myself obviously just not in this way

OUTSIDE THE FRAME

for Hannah Lowe

Dear Nelsa, please forgive my familiarity, but I don't know how else to begin. In the way of all photographs, you've become time's signature. Here, it is always 1955, and you, stalled in your 24th year. Sent this photograph by your niece, I have to confess I feel myself a trespasser. You are of my grandmother's generation of Caribbean women. This portrait you sat for, I know to be an older convention. Though I am sure you once (always?) believed in the dream of love, parcelled in the dedication you've penned to your beloved on the back. In your placid gaze, I see a willed-perhaps contentment (but what of the washing left on the line, your hope to return in time to gather it before rain set in?). In your half-smile, your eyes pointedly focussed away from the camera, you are the image of propriety (what of the dance floors, verandahs, and bedrooms of your life?). Scanning downward, what catches my eye are the details of the jacket you selected. Its collar, the slant of the lapel, and buttons all unmistakably conjure China. So, when now I return to your face – as with my own, your niece's, so many of the women of our country – I see again: the body is evidentiary, sedimenting its history.

DOMESTIC INTERIOR

photograph of my grandmother at my age

There is nothing beautiful about a woman
sweeping. Her housecoat's faint striping
suggesting prison is too on-the-nose. Yet
the domestic is always a story. If you're lucky,
some days a romance with all the violins
you could want. Most, a slow burn where
nothing happens, but afternoon light
bears down, its raiment a procession of days.

The body is averse to hoarding even
the casual violence of our misseeing. So,
in this photograph, don't look at the woman
futilely sweeping but at the vase, the flowers
she's carefully arranged. And thank them,
for God's sake, for their lack of utility.

CHIAROSCURO

I still don't know what here is the dark what part the light

LITTLE GIRL WHAT HAPPENED TO YOU
Four Pomegranates, Hope Brooks

it turns out a girl can live forever
cloistered in a courtyard bounded by walls
by frangipani sunlight and air thick
with approaching rain what made her
run here estranges her from herself
while the sea carries on with its residue
of salt on her reticulated skin
meshes in her hair coils and crashes in
cresting like the chorus in her head
noGodplease before falling again God
it seems has forsaken her yet she keeps
pressing together her palms asking silence
to wash over her blot out what pursues her
memory still meaning to overtake her

FEMICIDE
Resurrection, Joan Snyder

you cannot wear a red dress
when rape and murder have sewn it
so must document it piece it into
sequenced panels that recount violence
disproportionately wrought against
girls and women with a didactic hand
you must remand each newspaper story
to the custody of our view cut them
to scraps paste them into collage thusly
to make a mosaic of massacre
so we might measure ourselves
with a pattern to discomfit us you must
wield red in gash-like strokes slashing
accounts of each attack graffitiing
over the graphic details of each crime
you must believe if you array
events in this way we might arrive
on the other side of night and the final
canvasses you paint that open
unto blue and yellow will be the equal
of light and day will become
the resurrection possible if not in life then
in art this narrative arc you have arranged
for us to behold this arraignment
where savagery is not every time
a given not every time given
the closing argument

STUDY OF THE OBJECT

Near Chinatown, at the intersection waiting for the light, an older Chinese woman blurts out, "Nice dress. 4 or 6?" "Oh, I used to be a 6," she says when I confirm her guess, "now I'm an 8 or 10." Chagrin lingers in the air, and I want so badly a rescue from the body, endless object of scrutiny, our own often the most merciless. I want desperately to find a way out of this mess or some thread to seam our fraying social exchange, so offer, "I too sometimes wear an 8," though amend this in my head, as the light changes and I step off the curb, *in truth I've been everything from a 2 to a 20 but what the hell am I even saying look at us two women old enough to know better and what in God's name are we still doing*

IN MIDDLE AGE I WANT TO MEDITATE ON BLUE

no actually I want to be
every blue every possible
shade of sky and water want
to birth myself
into blue that wends
unbridled distancing
land from land the kind
that binds and compels
stunning us till we drown
in wave after wave
of our disavowals of faith
the kind of blue so blue
it does not care actually
for our seeing or
what we believe exists
nowhere really cannot
be found in the loveliest
of periwinkle winking
from a blush of petals
not in indigo sharpening
its knives not violet veering
toward mercurial midnight
not even in hopeful robin's egg
all of them just tricksters
no no other blue
will do at this late hour
but the original metaphysical
with her come-hither ways
dyed into the woven cotton
swishing between my legs
whoring me all the summers
of my days holding
my sex and death in check

THE NUDE

I grow weary of not using the word cunt.
Hers is the hairy mess I want, precisely that cunt.

Don't offer me a neatly trimmed or, God forbid,
shaved, depilated, waxed, exfoliated cunt.

I disavow the ones still posing as virgins,
won't suffer lightly those ever-prepubescent cunts.

Nor even wyfe or witch, reeking of myth, burned
for the crime of possessing her human cunt.

The one I need, the one I'm calling on now, is she
of the cuntiest-ways-of-knowing-herself cunt.

She, the alpha and omega, unshackled
by the chaos of the universe cunt.

She, the OG, motherfucking cunt come
to rain down fire on all our cuntishness.

CRAQUELURE

how fitting I would become more
by being less over time
cracked lines a webbed netting
patterns the surface of my skin
now I can begin to be beautiful
left with this gift
the evidence of my ravishment

WHAT'S YOUR FAVOURITE PIECE

One museum guard replied not directly to my question but indirectly that she likes the East Wing, where we were standing. As someone who has to be in a space for long hours, she prefers when she's assigned there: because of the light, she explained. Her colleague (they'd been chatting when I approached) said she prefers the West because she likes the French painters.

Another guard, in a different gallery of the same East Wing, told me of a painting I should look for in the West: two dogs searching for someone in a mountain pass, trapped in snow. He came to appreciate it, he said, after overhearing a docent addressing a group and learning its backstory. He couldn't remember the title or the artist's name but hoped I would still be able to find it from his description.

In a different museum, I spoke for at least fifteen minutes with B., the longest conversation I had with any museum guard in all my travels. She offered two answers: Renoir's *Luncheon at the Boating Party* and Lawrence's *Migration Series*. When I asked why those, she spoke less about the art and more about her experience of living as a child in the neighbourhood where the museum is now. She told me of her great grandmother, who took her to the museum often and told her to be sure she didn't act like she'd never been nowhere.

In another part of the same museum, an hour later, I posed the question to D. His selection echoed B.'s first: *The Boating Party*. Why? Because he loves Impressionism, he replied, then volunteered he too was a painter and pulled out his phone and shared with me some of his work.

What I haven't explicitly said, though maybe you've already intuited, is that I was in Washington D.C. and all the guards in this story were young Black women and men, except B., who was older than the others and older than me. What I also haven't said is I don't know if any of them figured out while we were talking that I'm also Black.

IN THE ARTIST'S STUDIO

Picasso's Studio, Faith Ringgold & *Tar Beach 2*, Faith Ringgold

in the centre of this room you are the nude in repose positioned
to look beyond the great painter shambled into a corner facing
the blank canvas trying to capture what still eludes him the
African forms that charmed him women's bodies those lighter-
hued he abstracted whereas your own is mahogany richly-fleshed
you the model and artist remaking herself

Faith

years ago I looked at your quilts with my daughters on my lap
while the stars fell down now again seated cross-legged on this
museum's floor I gaze up to your canvas hoping to quiet
the din of the world outside the borders you've sewn though
failing please know I hear your voice in this room cracking open a
window through which I too have crawled

AT THE NATIONAL GALLERY EAST
Sentinel, Simone Leigh

You are who I've come here to see.
Positioned at the entrance, as if guarding it,
your Black body rises up, in relief
sprawls your shadow across the museum's
white-grey marbled floor and walls.
Your form – *como una guitara,*
like mine – I think, before catching myself.
You were forged in the sculptor's imagination
as clearly other than me: your head,
a parabolic antenna, delicately balanced
atop an elegant, elongated neck; breasts,
so upright they belie gravity and time.
And your onyx skin shimmers night's palette.
At five or six, one of my daughters asked,
"Tell me again who in our family is Black?"
And after I catalogued, she gleefully announced:
"I'm like you, Mummy! Black on the inside,
white on the outside," race being a puzzle
she was self-satisfied to have solved,
until, some months later in school,
her teacher taught about King and segregation,
and she came home anxious again. I tried
reassuring, telling her something I knew
wasn't the whole truth: "That was the past."
But she kept worrying her line of questioning.
"If we had lived in that time, who would I
have had to go with, you or Daddy?"
What did my child know then of race?
Maybe everything I still don't.
Sentinel, who here are you guarding,
what are you guarding us against?

YET EVERYWHERE THERE ARE BIRDS

Airshaft, Nekisha Durrett & *Migration Series*, Jacob Lawrence

Durrett's glasswork frets Art Deco,
each panel chattering in my mind's ear
with Lawrence's Migration. Not birds
but the voices of those forced to leave
have trailed me here. Loss, their timbre,
even as the artist scaffolds a bridge
between past and present for us
to walk across. *Loss, loss, loss* settles
in my chest and feet, its three-part
measure, each beat, insists on repeat.
In the work's enclosure, yellow glass
filters sun. Light and Durrett's design
conspire to implicate us in her art.
Ironically, I think, intensifying
my truest nature: *Yellow girl*
in a yellow room, I almost say aloud,
which strikes me as funny, then
quickly shifts register. In history,
as in art and this architecture,
I am undrawn. Moving on
to the installation's upper floor,
I enter and am momentarily flooded
with relief: at last, I am eclipsed!
But oh how soon I am forced to see
I am now simply awash in blue,
my every hue undone by blueing
glass, this blued room casting,
defiantly, over me, its blue mood.

WHERE DOES A CANDLE GO WHEN IT BURNS
40 Acres: Camp Barker, Sandy Williams IV

By now it is long gone, the flames having consumed
the waxen Lincoln, seated in that pose made famous
by the version of him on the Mall, replicated, relocated
to this site and sculpted from material meant to perish.

On a D.C. street at dusk, I stood to watch the statue burn.
Perhaps it never existed, returned to its original state,
carbon dioxide and water evaporated into the ether,
this art that resurrects the dead with a decomposing eye.

What the artist memorialises is a habit history can't kick.
How many remember Camp Barker, Civil-War-era grounds
that housed formerly enslaved and free Black Americans?
I don't know where a candle goes when it burns, but I know

what it leaves behind is soot, shading promises unkept,
what it means to be a refugee in your own country.

SOMETIMES ANOTHER STAR CHOOSES

Sloop: Eldaz Crossing, Reggie Burrows Hodges

and she charts a shore visible
only to her the scale of her
immense she lords
over the sea and its spectral
elements commanding air
quelling the coming storm's
sulphurous clouds
with the slightest order
she disarms the waves
aligns currents straddling
the vessel above which she towers
her white dress billowing into sail
her legs fused to the hull she
captaining this crossing

IN THE ARTIST'S STUDIO

On a morning in November of 2023, I arrived at the artist's studio, housed in an old industrial warehouse converted into art spaces. We'd met when we were paired for a talk centred on our work as Black women artists responding to the history of the 18th-century. Covid forced the event online, and I lost the chance to see her paintings in person. Three years later, I reached out and asked if I could visit.

For my viewing, she'd arranged several of her paintings around the periphery of the room: some from the series I'd seen digitally in 2020 and others from a series in progress. I'd gone expecting to respond to what had prompted the trip, but the new paintings were what I was most drawn to that day. Over the course of a couple hours, I recorded my impressions and asked about the work, jotting snippets of conversation I later fleshed out.

Many contemporary artists seem to prefer nontraditional forms. I know you work in some of these as well, but painting feels to me central to your practice. Why painting for you?

The Western canon of painting is a presence that imposes its history and authority, which I see as a block to work around. Unlike many painters, I'm not interested in issues of perception and light. My painterly hand is fantastical. The flora in these paintings are symbols. Asters, for example, are migratory plants and intensely needed pollinators.

What are your influences as a painter?

Kindred by Octavia Butler. Earlier influences were pulp sci-fi comics, which I read growing up and would spend a long time staring at the covers. I was a latchkey kid and also watched a lot of TV. The colours, images, and what the medium itself looks like shaped my imagination.

What underpins your new series?

"American" in the title means not just the US but the larger Atlantic space, which brings in water. I'm interested in the history of colonialism, tied to slavery and ecology. As with some of my earlier work, I'm again using archives in this new series. The French wallpaper, the Equiano bust, and other unnamed busts from classical antiquity, which I've worked into these paintings, are images I've seen in archives in person, not sourced from the internet.

A good deal of research informs the images you paint. What do you think of the gap between what you know of the history of these images and what a viewer might?

I don't think of the relationship between the research I do and what I paint as being symmetrical, and I'm not interested in art that is didactic. My goal is to allow people to know something they don't know they know.

A HISTORY OF COLOUR

American Lawn, Alex Callender

Once leeched from lapis lazuli, now
chemically-derived, named ultramarine
blue, the most beautiful colour
is the one that doesn't exist. The painter's
pigments, her selection of synthetic tints hint
at the roots of cobalt, cerulean, and azurite –
opulent, lushly expressed in larger-than-life
asters and big blue stem and marsh cord grasses
overgrowing the field filling-up this canvas.
Close-ups of purple-blue flowers showcase
their black centres, massing a galaxy of stars.
Here and there, cyan blossoms erupt
into flame. The sky above all this modifies,
darkening the palette while hueing it mauve,
with dash-like strokes that conjure a meteor
raining down. Everywhere, there are
intimations of danger and grandeur,
an abundance of nature that feels utterly
unnatural. On an indigo river running
through this lurid lawn, colonial relics bob:
pages torn from an 18th-century book
of botanic drawings, chipped teacups,
a submerged, disembodied plaster head.
All are phantom presences, haunting
the surreal landscape of history's graveyard.

LANDSCAPE
The Thread of Colour, Maro Gorky &
Maro Gorky: The Thread of Colour, Cosima Spender

when I look out my window
memory comes between
me and the view

FOR BEAUTY IS NOTHING BUT THE BEGINNING
OF TERROR
A Scene from Anthropocene No. 2, Andrea Chung

the lionfish were never meant to be
where they've proliferated whole
species subjected to forced migration
rendering the sea irreconcilable
for native fish for reef survival
what is to become of us
I imagine the sea would cry out
if it could testify but greed
that old antagonist with so little
faith in time's long arm its reach
bequeaths the nightmare we keep
dreaming in the Anthropocene
when the sea is laced with cyanide
but oh it's beautiful in cyanotype

I WOULD LIKE TO KNOW WHAT THE RIVER KNOWS
River Scene, Henry Daley

how it washes boulders or smooths as it runs
rivelling earth I'd like to know the single tree
that finds succour here how it grows of soil
constantly shifting flooded by minerals
and what of the geometry between tree
and riverbed or of the tree's reaching for the dark
outline of mountains that seem to hold up the sky
not bluest at this hour but shot through
a scattering of reddening clouds overhanging
this sky a cut-out filigree of branch and leaf
triangulated shadow and light
and no human in this scene to disrupt
but me my imposing eye scrawling
the violence done on this land to this land

LAND THAT HAS NEITHER BEGINNING NOR END

Bosque de Pacho/The Forest of Pacho, José María Velasco

These woods, like mountains do, keep
legends alive. Skein of greens flecked
with ochre and brown permit my eye
to part leaf from bark, soil from grass.
Even without a fixed horizon, I orient
myself in this Eden: dense foliage
yet untrampled. The painting's
label describes, so frames the scene
as *claustrophobic*. But I disagree
with who directs us see the rampant
world as oppressive. Redolent memory –
forest humid with insect, tree frog
and bird call, chorus of wind
and night coming on – you return me.

HEAR MI NUH
Bush Have Ears, Everald Brown

True. Bush have ears, plenty
growing across hillside and valley,
in each plot awaiting harvest. But
Bush also have eyes that see past
all the greening. She,
with her labyrinthian ways, tendril
in every swath of land yearning
fi become sky, every tree that leaf
while grounding itself inna the soil.
Is Bush first teach we how
fi eat the flesh of the fruits
without imbibing poison. Seen?
Is she who know from time begin
all a we will face the fallowing.

WHAT BENDS TO THE BREATH OF ALL
VII. All Creation Held Its Breath. Ad Astra., Lina Iris Viktor

out of what ordains this savannah
she looks unto the new world and blazes
not yet hunter or hunted she is
set afire as the gold-leaf moon
too is lit by an unseeing hand
the universe conducting its wind
through her wired copper hair

YOU WANT TO WALK VERSUS DRIVE THROUGH
THE WORLD

is my husband's response when I return from one of my museum
trips lamenting I'm trying really trying but can't seem to make myself
love what I don't so much digital and installation work often leaves
me cold why do I keep returning to painting and drawing most

DEAR DADA AN ARS POETICA

Dear French *rocking horse*,
Dear Romanian or Russian *yes yes*,
Dear art that is whatever the artist
chances to make, to cast, to collect,
whatever the artist says it is,
including most often nothing at all.
Dear leaving it all up to the viewer,
Dear skirter of conversation, the (*gasp!*)
mere notion of communion (also Realism,
Impressionism, Expressionism, et al.).
Dearest *nada*, Congratulations!
You've succeeded so well. Achieved
your dream of the arbitrary. Irreverent
of nary an intent — except
of course irony — how very ironically
you've rendered yourself (for this viewer,
for what it's worth) virtually
irrelevant.

DOCENTS & POETS & OTHER INTERPRETERS

In a gallery featuring contemporary abstract art, a docent addressed a group of schoolchildren, ranging in ages ten to twelve. She instructed them to "draw whatever you want to sketch," as she distributed paper and pencils. This she followed with examples and elaboration on the exercise – "your dog, your house, whatever you want to express that's inside you" – though the images in front of them were clearly not of dogs or houses. As if overhearing my thoughts, she corrected: "You don't need to represent anything at all in 20th – I mean 21st – century art." *How do you express yourself without representing anything at all?* I am still puzzling over this.

In the incredibly crowded Van Gogh exhibit held in a different museum, it felt as if every patron was an art critic. In more than one conversation, I overheard a member of the party expounding on two aspects of Van Gogh's life that inflected, in their view, everything he painted: his mental illness and (now brought-into-question) suicide. No surprise. These parts, not the whole, of Van Gogh continue to circumscribe his images.

But haven't I also fallen under the sway of biographical interpretation, the tidy way it ties art to life? In my twenties, I too took liberties with the story of a man I did not know, invoking Van Gogh and two of his paintings to reckon with my father's own mental illness and suicide.

If even now I sidestep an artist's biography when writing poems engaging their art, I'm aware I'm still magnifying similarities and diminishing or even entirely ignoring differences between what they have created and what *I* want to talk about, to *express*. I interpret, as it pleases me. I riff and even grift. At its most electric, this writing is a quasi-collaboration, a (one-sided) conversation and improvisation, in which the moment of the art and my interiority spark and fuse. I don't know how to stop this from happening or if, in fact, this isn't the point.

OF CYPRESSES

Van Gogh's Cypresses, Vincent Van Gogh

Jagged stone walls look as if ravaged by storms,
though the cypresses remain upright.

> I must begin again to say what I see
> and not use the rotted names.

By daylight, one could send a soul safely
out into fields where cypresses loom.

> But why must I or how can I
> when all the names reek of their rot?

If the cypresses form an argument, it is neither
petition nor prayer. They appear never to weep.

> Then there's the matter of all this chatter.
> We all want a piece of you, Vincent.

Sentinels, they shoot upward in one painting,
swept into motion by the mistral.

> What exactly is a *mistral*? What does it say
> about me that I hear *mistress* and *minstrel*?

In another, they are barely but still there,
sequestered between farmhouse and mountain.

> That last one's rhetorical.
> I very much know what it says about me.

Even the madding yellow moon, the shock-lit
stars in nocturne frame them.

At this juncture, how much of my life have I
not begged, borrowed, or stolen from art?

I know I have no real claim to these trees.
Yet they have exerted some claim on me.

The better question is: how far will I go
in projecting myself onto everything I see?

THIS IS THE COLOUR OF MY DREAMS
Photo: This Is the Color of My Dreams, Joan Miró

this field flushed red glutted with the ever-present poppies a gaggle of them showing off then feigning the coquette amidst their verdant leaves but

oh oh oh

spotting the distance under the milkiest of skies slopes a pale yellow house I could enter and make a life

SELF-PORTRAIT: WISHING

For once in your life, just leave the dead stars
shuffling the dark. Don't you know nothing

is coming to answer your call? Sadness
is a doorstep, anytime now, you can quit

darkening. Why is it you still can't see –
you are just one spoke in the wheel?

No, you carry on thinking it's your job
to take every-last-one-and-god engine apart.

Always troubling the waters.
Can't leave well enough alone. If you would

stop flitting, stay put for one blasted second,
you might find some shards of the hope

for which you keep casting about. You might
figure out it's better to hang on to change,

burning a hole in your pocket, instead
of flinging it into a bottomless well.

OF GOATS & MEN
G.O.A.T, Again, Nari Ward

Come in like pure madness run amok.
Did people always fool-fool bad so?
Or maybe all of we just love fi fool weself.
I thought when goat laugh everyone
must go see him have no teeth.
But that truth like so many other
nuh seem fi hold water any longer.
I know is mi own madness mek mi
keep try fi spy a way through when none
in sight, is what mek mi go wheel
and turn and come again till mi draw
mi last breath. Still, is so mi give yu:
if yu let goat cavort inna yu field,
yu cayn surprise when him nyam it down.

INSIDE THE FRAME

Dear viewer, I know you want
the granular: all the details
not just the gist; the gristle,
the fat, not merely echo of bone.
You want the whole enchilada,
so to speak, and I'm truly sorry
to disappoint. When it comes down
to spilling the tea, the older I get,
it turns out, I'd rather not. Feel free
to chalk-up my shortcomings
to any or all: my misbegotten desires,
wishy-washy ways, or maybe
plain-old cowardice. In some instances,
on each count you'd be right. Yet
I hope it might alter your view a bit
to consider: like you, I too
despise many things. Example?
I never cared much for orange.
And now? Can't stomach the sight of it.
So must I traffic in that colour,
or any other, to prove my bonafides?
My politics? Such exertion,
despite best intentions, I've found
has a nasty penchant for shrivelling
not sharpening perspective.
If I could stand in any landscape
and with certainty sift
foreground from background, perhaps
the situation would be different.
But after years spent squinting
to see each image singularly,
clearly I've thrown in the towel.
Even now, I'm again confusing
the figurative for the literal –
a gift or curse, depending

on your purview, I suppose.
Goodbye and *hello*
mean the same in many a language
on this globe. If sadly not the idiom
in which I make my home,
I take heart in such coincidence,
the sometime-benevolence
of fate. I hope you might also,
dear viewer, and please,
if it pleases you, believe me
when I say: everything you imagine
I have stranded outside the frame
is bristling inside of it.

MANGO HEAD
Head, Alvin Marriott

Why yu always ask stupid question, ee?
The man call mango head because him head
shape like mango. What do yu anyway?
Yu come in with yu long face, gwyan
with yu sufferation parade. Yu nuh see
yu must either pick up yuself or put down
what yu cayn carry? Gal, is time
past time yu learn fi ban yu belly.

Is only when yu young yu can afford
fi believe the earth start spinning
when you one did step pon it. Cho. Things
always been hard, mi love, and if yu cyan
squinch-up yuself, at least you can try fi hear
what I telling yu: none of we invent the story.

THE ARGUMENT OF THE EYE
Red Composition, María Magdalena Campos-Pons

Red threads bind hands, enthrall,
loosely gather stalks of cane. Stalking
a face, red strings shutter eyelids,
wander closed lips, and drape
about the head, imposing a crown
on the one who bears its weight.
Where is this body bound?
By what oath now is it bound?
Red is the morning of blood —
in reedy streaks on arms or ribbons
through fingers wound, tracing
migration's routes, the invention
of borders and nations. Home,
one's identity, could be its tragedy.

SELF-PORTRAIT

I am what's called *Jamaica-white*
which is not a white Jamaican.

And into that difference of syntax
lies the difficulty of summing up history.

When I try to speak plainly
I find myself again at the proverbial shore.

As a child, I'm told I wandered our yard
in Kingston, head tipped as if I was listening

to the not-far-off sea or could cipher the wind.
I talked to fowl and expected their reply.

Maybe even then I was pursuing the wrong gods.
I know the moon, saddled by its rotation

around an all-consuming light,
cannot be other than a mirror. The problem

with every storytelling is that shorthand
too often becomes longhand.

If another grammar exists,
I still can only locate it

in the stilt-walking egret
wading through mangroves, in the air

after a storm and the slowing rain
pinging on a galvanise roof.

All the seconds like horses, gathering
their galloping hooves into my chest.

BETWEEN WHAT I SEE AND WHAT I SAY
Homeward, 2020, Arpita Singh

I want to go back home scrawled on a wash of blue *I want to go
back home* punctuates white boats floating small strips made of
the words *paper boat* or just *boat* a whole flotilla of them *I want
to go back home* repeats a warning to heed maybe for I know this
wanting how it capsizes and take several steps back back away
till the words disappear and what remains are the white-capped
waves in a sea on which a single black boat drifts

THE ROAD TO ZION

20th-century untitled painting by unknown Jamaican artist

To reach you must walk backwards,
past cane fields ravelling smoke.

Pay no mind to the girl-child, roadside
in her dutty dress, transfixed by the goat

struggling against its rope. She misplaced
her soul long ago in its bleating.

To avoid such a fate, you cannot dillydally,
but must keep moving till you cross over

duppy road and come to the house
of the blind woman, at the junction

of riverbed and mountain. Then
may you lift up your eyes and behold

the one who has been waiting
all this time for you to arrive.

∞ ∞ ∞

NOTES

This book engages with how we see and are seen, questions whose stakes are personal, philosophical, social, historical, and political – often several and at times all of these at once. Nearly all the poems in the collection are in conversation with visual art, the history of its making and specific pieces and exhibits I encountered in museums I visited in the US, in Jamaica, and in the UK, from July 2023 through April 2025. While I did not limit my viewing once I arrived, I chose the exhibits and museums I would visit based on my desire to put myself in front of works by Black, Caribbean, Latin American, and Women artists. At the outset of this book I was aware, as I remain, that much of how I learned to value art early in my life was shaped by looking predominantly at works created by European men. My goal was not to find a counterbalance so much as an opening and investigation of my own sightlines.

While working on this project, I consulted several articles and books by art historians and critics. Of those, Grace Aneiza Ali's *Liminal Spaces: Migration and Women of the Guyanese Diaspora* (2020), Jacqueline Bishop's, *Patchwork: Essays & Interviews on Caribbean Visual Culture* (2023) and *Relational Undercurrents: Contemporary Art of the Caribbean Archipelago*, edited by Tatiana Flores and Michelle A. Stephens, were especially helpful. There are two books of Jamaican Art gifted to me decades ago that I have read and looked at countless times in the interceding years, to which I also returned while writing these poems: Petrine Archer Straw and Kim Robinson's *Jamaican Art: An Overview with a Focus on Fifty Artists* (1990) and David Boxer and Veerle Poupeye's *Modern Jamaican Art* (1998).

For the individual artworks noted beneath titles of poems in this collection, I include here citational information, where and how I viewed each piece, and brief notes for further context in some cases. But there are many artworks that did not filter into this collection in one-to-one fashion, yet I know they impacted me and this book. Ebony Patterson's *Three Kings Weep*, which I viewed at the Portland Museum of Arts in Maine, as part of their exhibit *Fragments of Epic Memory* (October 6, 2023-January 7, 2024), springs to mind as just one example. I spent a great deal of time with Patterson's powerful and memorable work but did not ultimately respond with a poem. *Three Kings Weep* is a multimedia piece that includes an audio rendition of Claude Mackay's sonnet, "If We Must Die." Perhaps I felt poetry, not to mention a poem as tremendous as Mackay's, being embedded in the work itself was more than enough.

While I was grateful to expand my knowledge of art and learn of artists new to me through writing this book, it remains full of my occlusions. Containing countless omissions, it is not a compendium of art but a record of one person's attempt to see, at this juncture in her personal and our communal life. I hope a reader may be inspired to look up the artworks I cite, but I want to end by giving thanks to all artists – whether or not I call their names here and whether they are regarded as famous or wholly unknown – who make art and persist in doing so, especially now.

ARTWORKS

Hope Brooks' *Four Pomegranates* (1975). Mixed media on canvas. I looked at a photograph of this work many times in *Modern Jamaican Art* before viewing it at the National Gallery of Jamaica in Kingston as part of the permanent collection.

Everald Brown's *Bush Have Ears* (1976). Oil on canvas. I looked at a photograph of this work many times in *Jamaican Art: An Overview with a Focus on Fifty Artists* before viewing it at the National Gallery of Jamaica in Kingston as part of the permanent collection.

Alex Callender's *American Lawn* (2024). A series of paintings, primarily oil on canvas. I viewed the paintings in Callender's studio in Easthampton, Massachusetts in November 2023 while they were in progress. I am indebted to Callender for granting the use of *the invention of manageable space*, one of the paintings from this series, as the cover art for the Alice James Books/US edition of this book.

María Magdalena Campos-Pons' *Red Composition* (1997) from the series *Los Caminos* (*The Path*). Triptych of Polaroid Polacolor Pro photographs. I viewed this as part of *Behold*, a solo exhibition of Campos-Pons' work, at the Brooklyn Museum of Art in New York, September 15, 2023-January 14, 2024. While the idea for the title of my collection preceded my visit to the exhibit, I take pleasure in this echo. Discussing her process in a 2022 interview, Campos-Pons used the phrase "the argument of the eye," an allusion to the work of influential Victorian art critic John Ruskin, which I use as the title of my poem. In my poem I also borrow and paraphrase a line that serves as the title of another of Campos-Pons' photographic series and is integrated into the work itself, *Identity Could Be a Tragedy* (1995-96). I viewed this work too as part of the exhibit.

Andrea Chung's *A Scene from Anthropocene No. 2* (2016). Cyanotypes on 140 lb. watercolour paper. I viewed this as part of the exhibit *Sea Change*, featuring selections from the permanent collection of the Addison Gallery of American Art in Andover, Massachusetts, September 1, 2023-January 7, 2024.

Henry Daley's *River Scene* (1943). Oil on hardboard. I have looked at a photograph of this work for years in *Modern Jamaican Art*. I have viewed other work by Daley held by the National Gallery in Kingston but have never seen this painting in person.

John Dunkley's *Feeding the Fishes* (1940). Mixed media on plyboard. I have looked at a photograph of this work for years in *Modern Jamaican Art*. I have viewed many other works by Dunkley held by the National Gallery in Kingston, on permanent display in a room devoted to his work, but have never seen this piece in person.

Nekisha Durrett's *Airshaft* (2021). Two-story installation, translucent window film. To say I viewed this piece feels a bit inaccurate. I stood for a long time inside of it at The Phillips Collection in Washington, D.C. Durrett's installation was one of three works commissioned by the museum for their 100th anniversary in 2021.

Maro Gorky's exhibit *The Thread of Colour* (2025) and Cosima Spender's film, *Maro Gorky: Thread of Colour* (2025). I viewed this solo exhibition of Gorky's paintings at the Saatchi Gallery in London, May 23-June 8, 2025. I also watched the short film made by Gorky's daughter, documentary filmmaker Cosima Spender, which was part of the exhibit. Maro Gorky is the older daughter of artist Arshile Gorky, renowned for his work and role in the development of Abstract Expressionism. Credited by Maro for encouraging her early artistic development, Arshile Gorky committed suicide when she was a child. My poem rephrases and recasts one of Maro Gorky's statements about her work, taken from the documentary film by Spender.

Reggie Burrows Hodges' *Sloop: Eldaz Crossing* (2022). Acrylic and pastel on canvas. I viewed this piece as part of a solo exhibition of Hodges' work, *Turning a Big Ship*, at the Addison Gallery of American Art in Andover, Massachussets, September 1-December 31, 2023.

Albert Huie's *Crop Time* (1955). Oil on hardboard. I looked at a photograph of this work many times in *Modern Jamaican Art* before viewing it at the National Gallery of Jamaica in Kingston as part of the permanent collection.

Jacob Lawrence's *Migration Series*, odd-numbered panels (1940-41). Casein tempera paint on hardboard panels. I have viewed it many times at The Phillips Collection in Washington, D.C. as part of the permanent collection. The even-numbered panels, which I have also seen a number of times, are held by the Museum of Modern Art in New York.

Simone Leigh's *Sentinel* (2022). Bronze. I viewed it at the National Gallery of Art, East Building, in Washington, D.C. It was acquired for their collection after Leigh's hugely celebrated exhibition in the Biennale Arte 2022 in Venice, Italy. She was the first Black woman to represent the US in one of the oldest and most prestigious art events in the world, begun in 1895. The US has had its own pavilion at the Biennale since 1930.

Alvin Marriott's *Head* (1939). Mahogany wood. I looked at a photograph of this work many times in *Modern Jamaican Art* before viewing it at the National Gallery of Jamaica in Kingston as part of the permanent collection.

Joan Miró's *Photo: This Is the Color of My Dreams* (1925). Oil on canvas. I viewed this piece at the Metropolitan Museum of Art in New York as part of the permanent collection.

Lydia Panas' *Hidden Forest* (2023). Limited edition archival prints. I viewed the photographs as part of a group exhibition, *Sobre una mujer/About a Woman*, at the Art Museum of the Americas in Washington, D.C., July 27-October 8, 2023. I'm fortunate to have seen this show. Since taking office for a second time in 2025, Trump's sweeping executive orders have resulted in cultural bans and the defunding of many institutions that support art and artists. At the time of writing this book, two planned exhibitions at the Art Museum of the Americas had been summarily cancelled.

Pablo Picasso's *The Tragedy* (1903). Oil on wood. I viewed it at the National Gallery of Art, East Building, in Washington, D.C. as part of the permanent collection.

Howardena Pindell's *Memory: Future* (1980-81). Mixed media on canvas. I viewed it as part of the exhibition *Tender Loving Care*, featuring over one hundred selections from the permanent collection of the Museum of Fine Arts in Boston, July 22, 2023-January 12, 2025. As with Pindell's piece, many were newly acquired.

David Pottinger's *Street Scene* (1970). Oil on Canvas. I have looked at a photograph of this work many times in *Jamaican Art: An Overview with a Focus on Fifty Artists*. I have viewed other work by Pottinger held by the National Gallery in Kingston but have never seen this painting in person.

Bony Ramirez's *Machetazo!* (2021). Acrylic, color pencil, soft oil pastel, dulled machetes, and Bristol paper on wood panel. I viewed it as part of the exhibition *Tender Loving Care*, featuring over one hundred selections from the permanent collection of the Museum of Fine Arts in Boston, July 22, 2023-January 12, 2025. As with Ramirez's piece, many were newly acquired. I am indebted to Ramirez for granting the use of this piece as the cover art for this book.

Faith Ringgold's *Picasso's Studio* (1991). Acrylic on canvas and printed and tide-dyed fabric. I viewed it at the Worcester Art Museum in Massachusetts. Part of their permanent collection, it was included in a solo exhibition of Ringgold's work, *Freedom to Say What I Please*, October 7, 2023-March 17, 2024. The exhibit also included *Tar Beach 2* (1990). Screenprinted silk plain weave, printed cotton plain weave, synthetic plain weave, quilted. *Tar Beach 2* is one of a series of five "story quilts" depicted in Ringgold's children's book *Tar Beach* (1991). The book begins, "I will always remember when the stars fell down around me," which I paraphrase in my poem.

Alison Saar's *Blonde Dreams* (2021). Woodcut and screenprint on Okawara paper. I viewed it as part of the exhibition *Tender Loving Care*, featuring over one hundred selections from the permanent collection of the Museum of Fine Arts in Boston, July 22, 2023-January 12, 2025. As with Saar's piece, many were newly acquired.

Arpita Singh's *Homeward*, 2020 (2020). Oil on board. I viewed it as part of *Remembering*, the first solo exhibition of Singh's work outside of her native India, at the Serpentine Gallery North in London, March 20-July 2, 2025.

Joan Snyder's *Resurrection* (1977). Oil on canvas with collage of textile fragments and papers and mounted newsprint on plywood with paint, papier mâché, and mixed fibre board. I viewed it as part of the exhibition *Tender Loving Care*, featuring over one hundred selections from the permanent collection of the Museum of Fine Arts in Boston, July 22, 2023-January 12, 2025. Snyder's eight-panel, large-scale work was acquired in 1986 but only put on display for the first time in 2023.

Sheida Soleimani's *Banner Project* (2023). Photographs. I viewed these as part of the "Banner Project", featuring commissioned work by various contemporary artists, at the Museum of Fine Arts in Boston, August 20, 2023-June 23, 2024.

Vincent Van Gogh's *Van Gogh's Cypresses* (1853-1890, artist's life). I viewed this exhibition at the Metropolitan Museum of Art in New York, May 22-August 27, 2023. The ubiquity of Van Gogh's art means I have been able to see and revisit a great many of his paintings, at many major museums over the past three decades, including the Van Gogh Museum in Amsterdam. The Met exhibit featured over forty of his paintings and drawings, centred on the cypress trees to which he repeatedly returned.

José María Velasco's *Bosque de Pacho/The Forest of Pacho* (1875). Oil on canvas. I viewed the painting at the National Gallery of London as part of *A View from Mexico*, March 29-August 17, 2025. The monographic exhibition was the "first UK in-depth exploration of Velasco's work and the first ever dedicated to a historical Latin American artist at the National Gallery."

Lina Iris Viktor's *VII. All Creation Held Its Breath. Ad Astra.* (2022). Pure 24-karat gold, acrylic, copolymer resin, and print on cotton rag paper. Viktor's work was part of a group exhibition *Worlds Within and Without: An Exhibition of Contemporary Black Art* at The Madison Art Collection of the Lisanby Museum in Harrisonburg, Virginia, September 18 - December 7, 2024. The exhibit was opened in conjunction with the 2024 Furious Flower Black Poetry Conference, in which I was taking part. Unfortunately, Viktor's piece arrived after the conference ended and I was unable to return in time to see it in person. I viewed a digital image.

Nari Ward's *G.O.A.T., Again* (2017). Series of twenty sculptures. The sculptures were exhibited at Socrates Sculpture Park in New York, April 29-September 14, 2017. I did not see them then but have viewed digital images on the artist's website. Ward's series is a play on the acronym G.O.A.T. – Greatest of All Time – with reference to the culture of sport and more perniciously to Trump's rhetoric.

Sandy Williams IV's *40 Acres: Camp Barker* (late September-October 4, 2023). Beeswax. I viewed the first iteration of the Lincoln sculpture, part of Williams' ongoing public installation project *40 Acres Archive: The Wax Monument Series*. The first Lincoln was razed so quickly Williams later created a second (February 15-August 20, 2024), with fewer wicks to allow it to burn more slowly. I happened upon the first version of the sculpture in a square in Washington, D.C. on October 2, 2023. It was removed on October 4, 2023.

POEMS & MUSIC

The title of my poem "Of Goats and Men" alludes to Robert Burns' "Ode to a Mouse", written in 1785. Burns' poem contains these often-quoted lines, if usually heard in English rather than the original Scots: "the best laid schemes o' Mice an' Men/Gang aft agley/An' lea'e us nought but grief an' pain/For promis'd joy!" As an undergraduate, I had the great gift of learning from scholar Kathryn Freeman (1958-2025), with whom I took multiple courses on the British Romantics. Kathy remains one of my most influential and beloved teachers. This poem is dedicated to her memory.

The title of my poem "Sometimes Another Star Chooses" is taken from the opening line of Lucille Clifton's poem, "Leda 2," part of her series of three "Leda" poems (*The Book of Light*, 1993).

The phrase "poor me Israelites" in my poem "How Often Do You Return" is from Desmond Dekker's song "Israelites." Originally released in Jamaica in 1968, it went on to become an international hit in the UK and US.

Marta Gentilucci's *moving still: processional crossings* was commissioned by La Biennale di Venezia (2021). Poets Elisa Biagini, Irène Gayraud, Evie Shockley, and I collaborated with Gentilucci, composing texts we later recited in the premiere of the piece on September 23, 2021, at the Biennale in Venice, and in a performance a year later, on September 18, 2022, at the Paris Philharmonic. The poem "Passage" began to take shape in my mind, following a conversation with Gentilucci over Zoom in the spring of 2020, in which she shared her vision for the composition with me, Biagini, Gayraud, and Shockley. "Passage" was written over the course of the last two weeks of December 2020 with near daily Zoom conversations between me and Gentilucci as I developed it. It is in debt to Dante's *Inferno* and the stories of Persephone and of Orpheus and Eurydice and very likely other old texts and tales I am unconsciously drawing upon or confabulating in my poem.

One of the epigraphs for this book is drawn from Medbh McGuckian's poem "The Colour Shop" (*Captain Lavender,* 1994).

The title of my poem "For Beauty Is Nothing But the Beginning of Terror" is taken from the opening of Rainer Maria Rilke's poem, "The First Elegy" (*The Duino Elegies*, 1923).

The thirty-second section of Wallace Stevens' long poem, "The Man with the Blue Guitar," begins with these lines: "Throw away the lights, the definitions,/And say of what you see in the dark/That it is this or that it is that,/But do not use the rotted names" (*The Man with the Blue Guitar and Other Poems*, 1937). I allude to these in my poem, "Of Cypresses." Stevens' poem is also an example of ekphrasis.

ACKNOWLEDGEMENTS

I extend my sincere gratitude to these poets who give generously of their time as editors – Ronald Spatz, Faith Hill & Walt Hunter, Adam Piette & Alex Houen, Rebecca Lindenberg, Lauren Alleyne, Gerald Maa & Noah Baldino, Chloe Garcia Roberts & Major Jackson, Ron Slate, Camille Dungy, Laura Fyfe & Chris Powici, Jenny Molberg, John Skoyles, Adrian Matejka, Keetje Kuipers & Bill Carty, Hannah Lowe, Jessica Faust, John Whale, Emily Rosko, and Mia Leonin – and all the other staff members of the literary magazines in which poems in this collection first appeared, at times in earlier versions:

Alaska Quarterly Review, *The Atlantic*, *Blackbox Manifold*, *The Cincinnati Review*, *The Fight & The Fiddle*, *The Georgia Review*, *Harvard Review*, *On the Seawall*, *Orion*, *Paperboats*, *Pleiades*, *Ploughshares*, *Poetry*, *Poetry Northwest*, *The Poetry Review*, *The Southern Review*, *Stand*, *swamp pink*, and *SWWIM*.

Thank you to everyone involved with the publications, exhibits, and compositions, in which poems in this collection were also included:

"Domestic Interior" was featured in *Poem of the Day*, a project of the Poetry Foundation.

"Outside the Frame" will also appear in Hannah Lowe's *The Woman in the Chinese Collar*.

An excerpt from "Passage" appeared on *Poem-a-Day*, a project of the Academy of American Poets, selected by guest editor Safiya Sinclair.

"Passage" also forms part of the lyrics of *moving still: processional crossings*, a composition by Marta Gentilucci.

An earlier version of "What Bends to the Breath of All" appeared in *Worlds Within and Without: An Exhibition of Contemporary Black Art*, a catalogue from the exhibit of the same name, featuring the artworks and poems in response, commissioned by Lauren Alleyne.

"Wilding" was featured on *Poetry Daily*.

"Wilding" was also reprinted in the *50th Pushcart Prize Anthology*, selected by poetry guest editors Jessica Greenbaum, Katie Farris, and Michael Waters.

Thank you to Edward Hirsch and the Guggenheim Foundation and to the heads of my department and my dean at Penn State University for the gift of time that supported the writing of this book.

Thank you to the many colleagues, students, and teachers, with whom I've been fortunate to be in community – at Penn State, Pacific, and elsewhere – whose shared belief in the value of art and intellectual pursuit gives me hope.

There are many other individuals to whom I owe a debt of thanks:

Firstly, to my editor Jeremy Poynting for his faith in me and tireless advocacy, and to Hannah Bannister and everyone at Peepal Tree for their tremendous work.

To Grace Aneiza Ali, Ilya Kaminsky, Hannah Lowe, and Tim Seibles for the generous words they offered this book & for their own brilliant work.

For conversations that inflected this book and bolstered me along the way & for their inspiring work as poets, artists, scholars, and curators my gratitude extends to: Jason Allen-Paissant, Lauren Alleyne, Ellen Bass, Elisa Biagini, Jacqueline Bishop, Rhony Bhopla, Malika Booker, Paul, Beth, & Nathan Burch, Alex Callender, Anthony Vahni Capildeo, Todd Davis, Kwame Dawes, Camille Dungy, Sita Frederick, Gabrielle Foreman, Irène Gayraud,

Marta Gentilucci, Yona Harvey, Justine Henzel, Julia Spicher Kasdorf, O'Neil Lawrence, Ann-Margaret Lim, Adrian Matejka, Tyler Mills, Rooja Mohassessey, Mervyn Morris, Mark Nesbitt, Penelope Pelizzon, Iain Haley Pollock, Jane Satterfield, Kris Sealey, Susan Seltzer, Charif Shanahan, Tanya Shirley, Evie Shockley, Safiya Sinclair, Nicole Smythe-Johnson, Adrienne Su, Brian Turner, Katieann Vogel, and Melora Wolff. And Mary Molinary, in loving memory.

For the above and for their bighearted and insightful reading of this book in draft form, thank you to: Terrance Hayes, Mia Leonin, Mihaela Moscaliuc, Chet'la Sebree, and Michael Waters.

Last, but furthest from least, endless gratitude and love to: my husband, my *b'shert*, for listening to me talk through this book & reading it with his discerning eye and for everything he is; my daughters, who are wonders I behold and to whom I am beholden; my inimitable mother, the other OG; my aunt, whose move to nearby Zion sparked a poem but most of all has enriched my life; my sisters, who also went through the storm; and all my other family members and friends.

ABOUT THE AUTHOR

From Jamaica, and of Jamaican and Venezuelan parentage, Shara McCallum is the author of seven books published in the US & UK, including *Behold*, *No Ruined Stone*, *Madwoman*, *The Face of Water: New and Selected Poems*, *This Strange Land*, *Song of Thieves*, and *The Water Between Us*.

McCallum's poems and essays have appeared in publications across the US, Caribbean, Latin America, Europe, and Asia. Her poems have been translated into Spanish, Italian, French, Romanian, Turkish, Chinese, and Dutch; have been set to music and performed in venues including the National Opera Center of America, Venice Biennale, Paris Philharmonic, and ECLAT Festival in Stuttgart; and have been featured in short films, public art projects, and installations.

Awards for her work include a Guggenheim Fellowship, Musgrave Medal, NEA Fellowship in Poetry, Witter Bynner Fellowship, Hurston/Wright Legacy Award for Poetry, OCM Bocas Prize for Caribbean Poetry, Sheila Margaret Motton Book Prize, Agnes Lynch Starrett Prize for Poetry, and the Oran Robert Perry Burke Award for Nonfiction.

McCallum delivers readings, lectures, and workshops throughout the US and internationally and has taught creative writing and literature for several universities. From 2003-2017, she was Director of the Stadler Center for Poetry and from 2021-22 served as the Penn State Laureate. Appointed a Cheney Creative Fellow at the University of Leeds for 2026-27, McCallum is an Edwin Erle Sparks Professor of English at Penn State University.

ALSO AVAILABLE

The Face of Water: New and Selected Poems
ISBN: 9781845231866; pp. 140; pub. 2011; £9.99

McCallum's poems reflect her rooting in a Jamaican experience unique for her childhood in a Rastafarian home filled with reckless idealism, the potential for profound emotional pathology, and the grounding of folk traditions. Her work has explored what it means to emerge from such a space and enter a new world of American landscapes and values. These poems establish her as a poet of deft craft (and craftiness), whose sense of music is caught in her mastery of syntax and her ear for the graceful line. She transforms the most painful and sometimes mundane details of life into works of terrible and satisfying beauty.

Madwoman
ISBN: 9781845233396; pp. 72; pub. 2017; £8.99

"These wonderful poems open a world of sensation and memory. But it is a world revealed by language, never just controlled. The voice that guides the action here is openhearted and openminded – a lyric presence that never deserts the subject or the reader. Syntax, craft and cadence add to the gathering music from poem to poem with – to use a beautiful phrase from the book, 'each note tethering sound to meaning.'"
—Eavan Boland

No Ruined Stone
ISBN: 9781845235239; pp. 90; pub. 2021; £9.99

No Ruined Stone imagines what might have happened if Robert Burns had sailed from Scotland in 1786, as planned, to take a job on a slave plantation in Jamaica. Supported by research, it is a subtle, multi-layered verse narrative, voiced mainly by the poet himself and later by his granddaughter, passing for white. The worlds it vividly presents beget reflections on creativity, history, slavery, race and many other issues. It is an exceptional work, a memorable achievement.
—Mervyn Morris